SERVING THE NATION
AS A BUFFALO SOLDIER

A HISTORY-SEEKING ADVENTURE

by Allison Lassieur

CAPSTONE PRESS
a capstone imprint

Published by Capstone Press, an imprint of Capstone
1710 Roe Crest Drive, North Mankato, Minnesota 56003
capstonepub.com

Library of Congress Cataloging-in-Publication Data is available
on the Library of Congress website.

ISBN: 9781669069423 (hardcover)
ISBN: 9781669069393 (paperback)
ISBN: 9781669069409 (ebook PDF)

Summary: YOU are a Buffalo Soldier. You've joined the United States Army
and will soon serve the country you love with the rest of your all-Black regiment.
But Buffalo Soldiers faced many dangerous enemies—bloody warfare, sneaky
bandits, wild animals, and racism. What will you do as a Buffalo Soldier? Step
back in time to face the dangers and decisions brave Black men faced in their
fight to safeguard America.

Editorial Credits
Editor: Alison Deering; Designer: Bobbie Nuytten; Media Researcher: Jo Miller;
Production Specialist: Whitney Schaefer

Consultant Credits
Catherine Johnson Adams, associate professor of history, SUNY Geneseo

Image Credits
Alamy: Historic Images, 33, Pictures Now, 72; Getty Images: Archive Photos, 36,
freestylephoto, 22, Interim Archives, 18, MPI, Cover, 40; Library of Congress,
8, 89; Shutterstock: Everett Collection, 100, Kris Wiktor, 44, Kyle Krakow, 82,
Martina Birnbaum, 76; Wikimedia: Denver Public Library, 4, US National Park
Service/Fort Davis National Historic Site, 31

Printed and bound in China. PO 5827

TABLE OF CONTENTS

ABOUT YOUR ADVENTURE

YOU are a Buffalo Soldier. You've joined the army and will soon see the country you love! You might find yourself on a battlefield filled with smoke and gunpowder. Or you could be deep in the wilderness of a national park, defending the land from poachers. Wherever you find yourself, you fight—or die—alongside your fellow soldiers, all brave Black men.

Chapter One sets the scene. Then you choose which path to read. Follow the directions at the bottom of the page as you read the stories. The decisions you make will change your outcome. After you finish one path, go back and read the others for new perspectives and more adventures.

Turn the page to begin your adventure.

CHAPTER 1

DEFENDING AND SAFEGUARDING AMERICA

Black Americans have fought for America before it was even a country. Thousands of free Black men and formerly enslaved people fought in the Revolutionary War. More than 200,000 Black soldiers and sailors fought for the Union during the Civil War.

After the Civil War ended in 1865, the army formed units of all-Black soldiers. These regiments went west to protect settlements,

Turn the page.

guard travelers, and defend against attacks from Indigenous people. The Black soldiers in these regiments became known as Buffalo Soldiers. The nickname came from the Indigenous people of the American Plains. They thought the soldiers' dark, curly hair looked like a buffalo's coat. The name also meant something more—respect for their fierceness and bravery.

Buffalo Soldiers from the 25th Infantry at Fort Keogh, Montana

Buffalo Soldiers also had to battle a more dangerous enemy: racism. Everywhere they went, they faced hatred and suspicion. The military paid them less than white soldiers. They refused to allow Black soldiers to fight with white regiments. Black soldiers were assigned lowly jobs, far away from combat. Despite this hostility, Buffalo Soldiers proudly served from the late 1800s through World War II.

Do you think you have what it takes to be a Buffalo Soldier? Could you face bloody warfare, sneaky bandits, wild animals, and survive?

- To be a new Buffalo Soldier recruit assigned to a desolate desert fort in the 1880s, turn to page 11.
- To be a battle-hardened Buffalo Soldier sent to guard and protect Sequoia National Park in 1903, turn to page 49.
- To face terror as a Buffalo Soldier serving in World War I in 1918, turn to page 85.

CHAPTER 2

MISSION: PROTECT AND SERVE

You gaze at the endless desert stretching out to the horizon. You can hardly believe you're here—a free man and a soldier in the United States Army.

After the Civil War ended in 1865, you and all other enslaved people were freed. A year later, the U.S. Army created several all-Black regiments. The minute you heard about Black regiments, you enlisted.

For you and many other formerly enslaved Black men, joining the army made sense. There

Turn the page.

were very few jobs available to newly freed slaves. Becoming a soldier guaranteed food, clothing, a place to live, and a steady income. But there was something more. You felt pride in your country and wanted to be a part of it.

After weeks of training, your regiment is ready for its first assignment. The army has dozens of forts scattered throughout the Southwest. You might be sent to any one of them. You don't really care where you go. Being a free man in the army and serving your country are enough.

Your commanding officer appears. You and the rest of your regiment salute smartly, then wait for him to speak.

"I've been ordered to send soldiers to either Fort Grant in Arizona or Fort Davis in Texas," the commanding officer says. "Fort Grant is mainly guard duty. The commander needs extra men to form an armed escort to protect the paymaster. Each month he travels through the desert with a chest filled with gold and silver. This money is the soldiers' pay."

You think carefully. That money must be protected at all costs.

"At Fort Davis, you'll be on scout duty," the commanding officer continues, "as well as protecting settlers."

You nod. Fort Davis is a large military fort in a dry, dangerous part of Texas. You've heard reports of Apache attacks in that area.

The commanding officer eyes each of you. "You must be deployed to one or the other," he concludes. "But I'll consider any requests you might have."

- To ask for the Fort Grant assignment, turn to page 14.
- To request an assignment at Fort Davis, turn to page 32.

After several days of hard riding, you and the other Buffalo Soldiers arrive at Fort Grant. It's surprisingly large, with about two dozen buildings and barracks forming a *U* shape.

The commanding officer grants you a day to settle in. Then he assembles you and the others.

"Tomorrow you'll be escorting the paymaster to three other forts in this area," he begins. "He'll be carrying more than $28,000 in cash, silver, and gold."

Someone makes a low whistle at that staggering amount of money. The commander glares in their direction, then continues.

"This may seem like an easy job, but the area is crawling with outlaws and Apache," he says. "They mean business, and they're fearless. You must be on your toes at all times. Am I clear?"

You nod, suddenly feeling a bit apprehensive. You're embarrassed to admit it, but you did think this would be a quick, easy job. Now you realize you could die out there in the desert.

The next day, you set out with 10 other guards. The paymaster is riding in a sturdy, hard-topped ambulance wagon. In the back is the oak chest filled with gold.

The other guards ride in an open wagon. You're on a horse beside them, constantly scanning the area for any sign of danger.

Your destination—Fort Thomas—is about 60 miles away. The sun rises higher and hotter as the morning wears on. It's slow going on the rugged, rocky trail, and you use a red kerchief to wipe sweat from your face.

Suddenly a soldier shouts, "Someone's coming!"

Turn the page.

A Black woman riding a big horse appears on the trail. She's colorfully dressed in a yellow blouse, red skirt, and a floppy hat covered with paper roses and velvet streamers.

You grin, recognizing her as the wife of one of your fellow soldiers.

"Why if it isn't Frankie Campbell," you say. "What are you doing out here?"

"I was going to meet my husband at Fort Thomas," she says. "But I left something behind at Fort Grant."

"Why, that's 20 miles from here!" you exclaim.

It's far too dangerous for one person to be riding out here alone. Frankie needs protection if she's going to travel these remote roads.

- To escort her back to Fort Grant, go to page 17.
- To ask her to ride with your group to Fort Thomas, turn to page 20.

"I can't let you travel alone. Let me take you to Fort Grant," you offer.

Frankie agrees, and the two of you set off. For the next hour, you share lively conversation, and the time passes quickly. Unfortunately, you're too distracted to notice when a group of white men appears from behind a large cliff.

"Look what we have here," one of them says with a smirk. It's Gilbert Webb, mayor of the nearby town of Pima.

"What is your business, Mr. Webb?" you ask politely. Your hand slides toward your gun.

"I don't have to tell you nothing," Webb sneers. "You think you can order me around just because you're wearin' a uniform? You ain't worth anything. Your kind are nothing but cowards!"

"Now see here, Mr. Webb," Frankie begins.

Turn the page.

Buffalo Soldiers lead
their horses to water.

The white men point their rifles at you.

"You get out of here, Frankie," Webb says
in a low voice. "You don't need to see this."

You try to stay calm. "Do what he says."

Frankie looks at you in horror, her eyes wide
with fear for you. You swallow hard, then nod at
her to go. She gallops away in a cloud of dust.

One of the men grabs your rifle. "You're one of them guards for the gold wagon, aren't you?" he growls. "I saw you back at the fort. Lucky for us, it'll be one less guard to deal with when we go for that gold."

At that, you freeze. The man with the rifle jabs it in your back, and you stumble forward. The men drag you into a small hidden canyon where Webb ties your hands and feet together.

"No matter," he says. "We'll find that gold. But no one will find you!"

He turns to his gang. "Let's go!"

They all ride away, leaving you behind. Webb is right, no one ever finds you—not alive, anyway.

THE END

To follow another path, turn to page 9.
To learn more about Buffalo Soldiers, turn to page 103.

"Ride with us," you say. "We'll protect you."

Frankie agrees, and you set out again. The trail dips down a hill and through a narrow space between two small cliffs topped by trees. Suddenly the whole group comes to a stop.

"There's a boulder blocking the trail," one of the soldiers calls.

Sure enough, a huge boulder sits on the trail. There isn't enough room for the wagons to drive around it. The only way to keep going is to move the boulder out of the way.

"Men, get that big rock out of the way," you order. "If you all push, it won't take long."

The men all lay down their weapons and get to work. You can help them, or you can guard the wagon with the gold.

- To help with the boulder, go to page 21.
- To guard the wagon, turn to page 24.

You're impatient to get going, so you put down your own gun and start helping. As you work, you notice a pile of small rocks holding the boulder in place. An uneasy feeling tingles up your spine.

"Look here," you say. "This rock was put here by human hands."

You look up the cliffs. Without warning, several white men run out of the trees. They hold rifles in their hands.

"Get that gold!" they shout, opening fire.

It's a robbery! You have a split second to decide. Do you run for your gun and return fire? Or do you hide behind the boulder?

- To run for your weapon, turn to page 22.
- To dive for cover behind the boulder, turn to page 23.

Just as you dive for your rifle, a bullet tears through your leg. You grab the gun, yelling in pain as another bullet hits your shoulder.

You crawl to the wagon as pain shoots through your body. You must protect the gold! Dizzily, you try to aim at the figures along the cliff, but your eyesight grows dim. The rifle drops from your hands. You take your last breaths as your blood stains the desert beneath you.

THE END

To follow another path, turn to page 9.
To learn more about Buffalo Soldiers, turn to page 103.

You take cover and one of the soldiers hands you a revolver. You peer around the boulder and are shocked to see a familiar face. It's Gilbert Webb, the mayor of the nearby town of Pima!

You fire at several white men running toward the paymaster's wagon. One turns and fires at you, hitting you in the shoulder.

Bleeding, you stumble away and collapse. *This is it*, you think as things go dark.

When you wake, you're lying in the dirt with a bandage on your shoulder. The other soldiers tell you what happened: a band of white men led by Mayor Webb injured several soldiers and took off with the gold. You are loaded onto the wagon for the long trip back to Fort Grant. You hope you survive to testify against those thieving murderers.

THE END

To follow another path, turn to page 9.
To learn more about Buffalo Soldiers, turn to page 103.

The boulder doesn't budge. You stand in the open wagon and look along the cliffs. Suddenly several white men appear, yelling and shooting.

"Give us that gold!" one shouts.

You're astounded to see it's Gilbert Webb, the mayor of the nearby town of Pima. He clearly wants the gold for himself.

Heart pounding, you return fire. The other soldiers grab their weapons and scatter. Several men fall to the ground, shot by the bandits.

The gunfire panics the horses. They pull the wagon toward the cliffs. It overturns, and you fall out, landing on your arm with a crunch. Pain shoots up your broken arm. You need to get to cover. It's the only way to survive this shootout. There's a rock ledge nearby. Or you can crawl under the overturned wagon.

- To go to the ledge, go to page 25.
- To crawl under the wagon, turn to page 28.

You crawl through the desert dust as bullets whiz overhead. Finally, you make it to the ledge. Sergeant Brown, one of the best marksmen in your troop, is there, shooting at the bandits.

He aims and shoots, knocking one robber to the ground. Using your broken arm, you manage to fire. More bandits appear. You're running out of ammunition.

"I don't think we can hold out much longer," Brown finally says. He loads his last bullets into his revolver.

It's time to retreat or die. You pull your trigger, but it only clicks on the empty chamber. The robbers' bullets ricochet off the ledge as Brown empties his own gun. He drops it and grabs you. You're dizzy with pain, so he helps you climb over the back of the ledge and down the hill behind. A few other injured soldiers and the paymaster are there.

Turn the page.

Together, you crouch behind the hill as shouts and gunfire ring through the air. If the robbers find you, they'll kill you for sure. For the next hour, you pass in and out of consciousness. Finally, the gunfire stops. A soldier appears.

"They got it all," he says. "Every last cent!"

Then, to everyone's surprise, Frankie Campbell appears from around the cliff.

"Where'd you come from?" you croak.

She laughs. "I hid out. Good thing too! You boys need some help."

She splints your arm and gives you water. You manage to return to the wagons. Sure enough, the oak chest is empty. The uninjured soldiers manage to fix the harnesses and find the surviving mules and horses.

Sergeant Brown helps you and the other injured soldiers into the wagon for the ride back.

But a few are too badly hurt to travel. They won't survive the trip.

"I'll tend to them," Frankie offers. "I'm sure the fort's doctor will be here in no time."

"It's too dangerous!" you say. "Those thieving robbers might come back. Or you could get ambushed by Apache!"

"I'll be fine," Frankie says, dismissing you with a wave. "Just make sure those robbers and Apache don't get to you first!"

That's a sickening thought. Injured and out of ammunition, no one one would survive another attack. You say a prayer as the wagon lurches forward for the long trip. You're thankful that you're still in one piece, and you hope you stay that way.

THE END

To follow another path, turn to page 9.
To learn more about Buffalo Soldiers, turn to page 103.

It's safe under the wagon, and you have a good view of the bandits. Ignoring the pain in your arm, you aim and shoot over and over. It doesn't seem to stop the bandits. They get closer, returning fire and shouting curses and slurs.

You fire your last bullet. The bandits return fire, and a Buffalo Soldier slumps against the boulder. Blood pours from a wound in his leg. He sees you under the wagon.

"I'm a goner," he croaks. "Take my ammo, you need it." He tries to toss his ammo pouch to you. It lands several feet away.

You need that ammunition. With it, you can defend both yourself and the injured soldier. If you try to rescue him, you both might die.

- To get the ammo, go to page 29.
- To help the soldier, turn to page 30.

You scramble out from under the wagon and run, pausing to scoop up the ammo pouch.

Suddenly, a gunshot tears into your shoulder. You fall, screaming in pain and clutching the wound, waiting for a bullet to finish you off.

Strangely, there's no more shooting. Instead, shouts and laughter fill the air. The bandits have found the oak chest. You raise your head in time to see them smash it open with an axe and pull out bags of gold and silver coins. It's the last thing you see before your world goes dark.

You wake up at Fort Grant. You've got a broken arm and have lost a lot of blood, but you're alive. The other soldiers report that the bandits have been caught and will be brought to trial. You can't wait to see them get the justice they deserve.

THE END

To follow another path, turn to page 9.
To learn more about Buffalo Soldiers, turn to page 103.

The best thing you can do is to save yourself and as many of your fellow soldiers as you can. Heart pounding, you crawl out and run to the boulder. The other soldier is alive—barely.

You throw him over your shoulder and stagger toward a dry creek bed about 100 yards away. Bullets rip your sleeve to pieces, but somehow they don't hit you. Finally you collapse at the dry creek bed, safe and away from the fighting.

When you wake up, you're surrounded by several other injured soldiers. Frankie Campbell is there too.

"What happened?" you croak.

Frankie shakes her head "Those men got away with all the money. But I saw them. It was that thieving Gilbert Webb, the mayor of Pima. He was too dumb to even wear a mask!"

A reinactment of Buffalo Soldiers firing back during an ambush.

Another injured soldier says, "There'll be a trial for sure."

"There better be," you say.

You vow to do whatever you can to make sure the thieves are thrown in jail or hung. Either way, they'll pay for what they did.

THE END

To follow another path, turn to page 9.
To learn more about Buffalo Soldiers, turn to page 103.

Fort Davis is surprisingly comfortable for a military fort in the middle of the Texas desert. Dozens of long, low buildings stretch across the dry land to the rocky mountains nearby. The whole fort has gas lighting and running water. What luxuries!

Once you and the others have settled in, your commanding officer calls the scouts together.

"The Apache are led by Victorio, a great leader," he begins. "Their original home was the land surrounding Warm Springs. They consider the place to be sacred. A few years back, the government turned that land into a reservation."

It's unusual for the U.S. government to turn sacred lands into reservations and allow Indigenous people to live there. You've heard stories about the terrible conditions of some reservations.

Apache Chief
Victorio Chiricahua

"It was peaceful for a time," he continues.
"Then white settlers in the areas accused the
Apache of raiding and stealing. It's likely bandits,
not Apache, were responsible, but the damage was
done. The government ordered the Apache to a
terrible reservation miles from their sacred home.
Eventually Victorio had enough and declared war."

Murmers of shock fill the air. Although you're
loyal to the United States, it's hard to hear how
badly your government is treating the Apache
and other Native people.

Turn the page.

A look of sadness crosses the commanding officer's face. "Even though Victorio and his warriors are a danger, his people are also hungry and desperate. Your mission is to protect our settlers from attack and thievery. But be compassionate. Leave Apache women and children alone. Is that clear?"

"Yes, sir," you say.

The the other scouts nod in agreement. But some look as if they aren't going to listen. You'll have to watch carefully when you're on patrol.

The scouts will be split into two groups. One will head west to an area where Victorio was last seen. The other will ride east and check on some settlements.

- To go west, go to page 35.
- To go east, turn to page 40.

You head west to hunt for Victorio. For days, you ride through the harsh desert landscape. Each night, you find a watering hole where you can make camp. Some are big enough to swim in. Others hold only a small amount of rainwater.

The farther west you go, the more dangerous the land. Watering holes are hard to find.

One afternoon, a scout who's been riding ahead gallops back. He's found fresh hoofprints at the base of a dry, rocky mountain. You're sure Victorio and his raiding party were here.

The men argue. Some want to follow the trail. Others point out that you're low on water.

The decision is up to you. Do you follow the trail and hope you find Victorio before the water runs out? Or do you head back to the fort and report what you found?

- To follow the trail, turn to page 36.
- To return and report Victorio's location, turn to page 38.

One scout insists there's water in the mountains.

"I've seen the watering hole myself, sir," he says. "It's huge, and there's plenty of water in it!"

You nod, trusting him, and follow the trail.

The scouting party climbs for hours. The faint trail winds up steep, rocky slopes, then plunges into hidden crevices. It's so hot that you can't help but gulp the last of the water, knowing more is nearby.

Buffalo Soldiers lead their horses on a steep mountain trail.

Finally, the trail disappears altogether.

"The watering hole is just around that cliff, sir!" the scout insists.

You round the cliff, ready to dive into the cool water. Instead, you stare in horror at a muddy puddle of dirt and rocks where the watering hole used to be.

"I-I . . . I'm sorry, sir," the scout stammers. "It was fine, sweet water a month ago."

It's not his fault the watering hole dried up, but that doesn't matter now. The water is gone. You'll all die of thirst long before you make it back. All you can do is wait and hope someone finds you.

Unfortunately, no one does. You all die in the harsh, unforgiving wilderness.

THE END

To follow another path, turn to page 9.
To learn more about Buffalo Soldiers, turn to page 103.

It's disappointing to abandon the hunt for Victorio, but there will be other chances. After hours of riding, it's time to make camp. You and another Buffalo Soldier go to check out a nearby watering hole. As you approach, you hear voices.

Quietly, you dismount and crawl to the edge of the cliff. Below, several Apache surround the watering hole.

Your heart thumps with excitement. You've caught Victorio! Then you look more closely. The group is only women and children.

The other soldier lifts his gun, ready to fire. You grip his arm.

"No!" you whisper. "We obey orders. These people are no threat to us."

The other man is furious but lowers his gun. The group of Apache packs up and disappears in the desert sunset.

The next afternoon, you arrive at the fort to make your report. There's a new commanding officer—a white man—in charge, and he's furious.

"Your duty is to clear this area of all Apache," he growls. "Why would you let them go?"

You try to explain that they were women and children, but he doesn't listen.

"Your kind are too soft," he continues. "You're not fit to be soldiers. You're relieved of duty. You have 24 hours to get out."

The unfairness of his words make you sick to your stomach, but there's nothing you can do. You pack up and leave the next morning. It's a bitter blow, but you know you'll never regret your decision to let those Apache live.

THE END

To follow another path, turn to page 9.
To learn more about Buffalo Soldiers, turn to page 103.

You head east to check on several settlements. The settlers there haven't seen Victorio.

You're relieved that the settlers are safe but frustrated the Apache leader is still out there somewhere. You do hear rumors that a band of Apache have been seen near a large watering hole several miles away. It's decided to set up a hidden camp near the watering hole and wait.

One evening at sunset, a scout rushes excitedly into camp. "They're here!" he cries.

Buffalo Soldiers rest next to a fire after setting up camp.

Everyone grabs their weapons and quietly approaches the watering hole. Sure enough, a group of Apache and their horses are gathered. It's almost dark, but you see a man matching Victorio's descripton—solid build with long hair and a steady gaze.

Suddenly the Apache shout and jump on their horses, opening fire. You've been spotted!

A bullet whizzes past your ear. Before you can return fire, Victorio and his warriors disappear into the darkening desert.

"We have to follow them!" one Buffalo Soldier shouts.

Another Buffalo Soldier chimes in. "Those Apache know this land. We'll never find them at night. Best to wait until morning when we can see their trail."

• To follow the Apache, turn to page 42.
• To wait until morning, turn to page 44.

If you wait you may lose Victorio for good, so you give the order to follow. The party gallops across the dry landscape, confident that the Apache are close. But the desert is quickly plunged into inky darkness.

You have to admit this wasn't a great idea. "Let's turn back," you order. Reluctantly, the others agree.

The moon offers faint light, but it's not enough to see where you're going. Soon, you realize you're lost. The party rides into a small canyon you don't recognize. Then a gunshot rings out, and a Buffalo Soldier slumps off his horse and hits the ground.

Ambush! The Apache must have been following all along!

Suddenly, it's chaos. Men are shouting, and gunfire is all around. Your horse rears, throwing you to the ground. You jump up and fire blindly in the direction you think the attack is coming from. A bullet tears through your jacket and another shatters your arm. You collapse in a pool of your own blood.

The desert breeze feels cool on your face. It's the only thing you feel other than the warmth of your blood on your skin. Slowly you close your eyes and bleed to death, lost in the desert for good.

THE END

To follow another path, turn to page 9.
To learn more about Buffalo Soldiers, turn to page 103.

You return to the hidden camp to wait.
The men stay up late talking excitedly about
how they'll capture the famous Apache leader.

"I'll take first watch," you volunteer.

Everyone else falls asleep. The desert is
cold and quiet. The only sound is the wind.
You start to feel sleepy. You could take a walk
to stay awake. But it may be a good idea stay in
the safety of the campfire.

- To stroll around camp, go to page 45.
- To stay by the fire, turn to page 46.

As you walk, your heart aches with the beauty of the desert at night. This kind of freedom was only a dream when you were a boy on an Alabama plantation. Now you can go anywhere and do anything you wish.

Suddenly a sharp pain stabs your ankle, followed by another. Hisses and dry rattling noises fill the air. You've stepped on a rattlesnake den!

Screaming, you pull several snakes off you and fling them into the darkness. You limp back to camp. Your leg is covered with bloody fang marks. The scouts try to heal them by putting gunpowder and salt on the wounds. But it's hopeless.

Strangely, you're not afraid. You lay by fire and watch the stars. Then you close your eyes as a free man for the last time.

THE END

To follow another path, turn to page 9.
To learn more about Buffalo Soldiers, turn to page 103.

A shout wakes you. It's dawn. You can't believe you slept all night!

"Sir!" a scout calls. "They took all the horses!"

The horses are gone and so is most of the food. It must have been Victorio and his men! They also took weapons and ammunition.

White-hot anger rages inside you. How could you have been so careless?

The other Buffalo Soldiers curse and argue. At first, you yell too. But then a thought pops into your head. Victorio and his men could have killed you all in your sleep. Instead, they took what they needed and let you live.

Maybe the Apache aren't bloodthirsty like everyone says, you realize. Maybe they're just people who want to survive—like you were, when you were enslaved. The thought washes away the fury like cold water.

The scout reports you're closer to the fort than you realized last night in the dark. As you gather the remaining supplies, another thought hits you. This incident will likely end your army career. No officer will trust you again.

Sure enough, when you get to the fort, the commander is furious.

"You let Victorio make a fool out of the U.S. Army," he fumes. "We have no room for cowards like you. I expect you to be gone by dawn."

It's a bitter blow that leaves you feeling sick. You love the army and are a good soldier. You have no idea what you're going to do next. But as you pack, you remind yourself that no matter what, you'll still be a free man.

THE END

To follow another path, turn to page 9.
To learn more about Buffalo Soldiers, turn to page 103.

CHAPTER 3

GUARDING THE NATIONAL PARKS

You have been free all your life, but your parents were enslaved. They gained their freedom in 1865, when the Civil War ended. They worked hard to give you a safe home and a good education in a small Ohio town. But a restlessness filled your heart. When you were old enough, you joined the U.S. Army.

Luckily, you were assigned to the Ninth Cavalry, I Troop. The all-Black regiment is managed by Charles Young, the only Black army troop commander. In October 1902,

Turn the page.

the Ninth Cavalry is assigned to the Presidio, a large army fort in San Francisco, California.

You've only been there a few months when you get a new assignment: to guard and protect Yosemite and Sequoia National Parks. You've heard about the breathtaking beauty of the new national parks, established in 1890. Now you'll get to see it for yourself.

In the early summer, the regiment starts the 323-mile trip to the park areas. After 16 days of hard riding, you finally make it to Sequoia.

Commander Young immediately gets everyone to work setting up a camp. Once that's done, it's time to find out what work assignment you'll get.

"I need volunteers to oversee a road-building crew," he says. "You will be responsible for constructing a road to some of the most scenic areas of the park."

You nod thoughtfully. Road building is hard work, but seeing more of the park is appealing.

"I also needs soldiers to patrol the park," Commander Young says. "We've had trouble with poachers and fires, as well as some of the settlers who came here to farm. They've used the park's land to plant their crops and the meadows to graze their sheep since the 1880s—before this was a national park. Sheep farmers strongly resisted the creation of the park. For them, it meant losing grazing area."

You frown. You've heard that even now, 13 years after the parks were created, illegal grazing is still a big problem.

- To volunteer for road building, turn to page 52.
- To ride out with a patrol, turn to page 66.

Road building isn't the most glamorous job, but you don't care. You've dreamed of seeing a national park ever since you heard about Yellowstone National Park being established in 1872. Back then, the idea of exploring the wilderness as a free man was almost unimaginable. Now you'll be able to enjoy a park's beauty and improve it for others to enjoy. It's a job you're happy to do.

Right now, there's only one short, rough wagon road leading into the park. The crew will repair the road and extend it to the stunning sequoia trees.

Captain Young gazes up at a giant sequoia and smiles. "One day, hundreds of people will want to come here," he says. "Flat, safe roads will encourage people to explore."

Road building is backbreaking work. The crew cuts down trees, pulls stumps, clears underbrush, hauls wagonloads of supplies, and digs a level bed for the road.

There's so much work that Captain Young hires white civilians from a nearby town to join the crew. Most of the men are fine to work with. But a few don't bother to hide how they feel about working with Black soldiers. They refuse to work alongside you or share tools. Some mumble curses and names under their breath as you pass.

You decide to ignore it and focus on the job at hand. The lumber crew needs help cutting down trees. The wagon crew could use help hauling supplies from the main camp.

- To join the lumber crew, turn to page 54.
- To help the wagon crew, turn to page 61.

Every day, the lumber crew surveys the area where the new road will be built. You mark the trees to be cut. There are a few giant trees here, so you carefully plan to build the road around them.

Some days, you go out early to enjoy the forest alone. The woods are alive with birdsong. Insects buzz and dart through the still air. You breathe deeply and inhale the spicy scent of the forest.

One early morning, you spy two strangers among the trees. When you approach, they drop their axes.

"Morning," you greet them.

They don't say anything. A twinge of suspicion grows in your mind.

"I didn't know we had new crewmen," you say carefully.

"Yup," one of them replies. "Um, Captain Young hired us."

"That's right," the other said.

"What are you doing so far out here?" you ask. It's odd to find men working so deep in the forest. You're at least a mile from the construction.

The first man answers quickly. "We, um, our orders are to clear out this underbrush so it'll be ready for the crew."

You're quiet for a moment. Captain Young did order the crew to speed up their work. It's possible he hired extra workers to clear the forest and move things along. But surely he would have told you? You're not sure what to do.

- To leave the men to their work, turn to page 56.
- To keep talking to them, turn to page 58.

It's unlikely that poachers or thieves would know Captain Young's name, so you take the men at their word. You give them specific instructions on which sections to clear, then make your way back to the main construction area.

It's nightfall when the crew gets back to camp. You're so tired you crawl into your tent and go to sleep, the strangers forgotten.

The next morning, a fellow Buffalo Soldier shakes you awake. "Captain Young wants to see you," he says.

Quickly, you dress and head to the captain's tent. He doesn't look pleased.

"Did you speak to two strangers working in the woods yesterday?" he asks.

"Yes, sir," you respond. "They said you hired them to clear the forest for the new road. They knew your name, so I believed them."

"I didn't hire them," he says. "This morning we discovered several weapons and boxes of ammunition were missing. The evidence points to those men as the culprits."

You're filled with panic and shame. If you had done your duty and questioned them more closely, you could have prevented this.

Captain Young shakes his head sadly. "I don't think I can trust your judgment. I'm sending you back to the Presidio. Your time in the park is over."

THE END

To follow another path, turn to page 9.
To learn more about Buffalo Soldiers, turn to page 103.

You're sure Captain Young wouldn't have hired such shifty characters. Your suspicions are confirmed when one of the men bends to grab his axe. You see a revolver hidden under his shirt.

Fear prickles your spine. Every worker knows weapons aren't allowed in the park. These men could be poachers or thieves. Either way, you're in danger.

The first man straightens, his eyes narrowed with suspicion. He knows you saw his gun. The other man shifts his weight and puts his hands in his pockets. He must have a weapon too.

You need to be careful. It might be a good idea to let the men go and make an arrest later. Or you can do your job now and take their weapons and escort them to camp. This could be a life-or-death decision.

- To take their weapons, go to page 59.
- To let them go, turn to page 60.

"Weapons aren't allowed in the park," you say. "You'll have to come back to camp with me."

Several things happen at once. The first man reaches for his gun as the second man lifts his axe and swings. You drop to the ground as the axe whizzes over your head, barely missing.

Before the man has time to swing again, you scramble to your feet and throw him against a giant sequoia tree. He hits his head, hard, and his body goes limp.

You don't see the second man behind you as he lifts the gun and pulls the trigger. The bullet hits your neck. You crumple to the ground, feeling warm blood pulsing out of your artery. In your last moments, you stare upward at the mighty sequoia stretching into a tiny patch of clear blue sky.

THE END

To follow another path, turn to page 9.
To learn more about Buffalo Soldiers, turn to page 103.

"Oh, since you're new, you probably don't know that weapons aren't allowed in the park," you say carefully. "You'll need to take them back to camp. All weapons are stored there when not in use."

The men exchange dark looks. For a moment you think they might attack. But luck is on your side. They nod, then leave through the woods.

Immediately, you return to camp and report what happened.

"You did the right thing," Captain Young says.

He orders a security patrol to chase down and capture the men. You give them a good description, and they head off.

Smiling, Captain Young turns to you. "You protected the park and yourself. Well done."

THE END

To follow another path, turn to page 9.
To learn more about Buffalo Soldiers, turn to page 103.

Each morning at camp, you help load the wagons with supplies and tools. You enjoy the long ride through the forest to the road-building site.

The road you're working on leads to one of the most beautiful sequoia groves in the park. These massive trees grow hundreds of feet in the air. The biggest one in the grove is named the General Grant, after Ulysses S. Grant, Union commander and president of the United States.

Another wagon driver, Tom, is a white man. He refuses to speak to you or any other Buffalo Soldiers. You're used to this kind of treatment, but it doesn't make it easier. Still, you focus on the job at hand.

One morning, you get word that Tom's wagon has broken down somewhere in the forest. Do you help Tom, or do fetch someone else to do the job?

• To help Tom, turn to page 62.
• To find someone else to help, turn to page 64.

Even though Tom has been hostile, you choose to help. Following Captain Young's orders and finishing the road on time is all you care about.

"What's wrong with the wagon?" you ask when you arrive.

"I don't know," Tom replies shortly, looking annoyed. "I drive wagons, I don't fix them."

"Well, I do both," you say. When you find the broken part, you get to work.

Tom leans in. "How'd you learn that?"

"My father taught me," you reply. "He owns his own blacksmith shop."

Tom looks stunned. "You mean a Black man owns a business?"

"Yes, of course," you say as you finish the repair and gather your tools. "Many Black men own very successful businesses."

"That was fine work," Tom mumbles, clearing his throat. "There's a game of cards at my tent after supper. Eight o'clock."

You're shocked at the invitation, but you accept. For the rest of the summer you and other Buffalo Soldiers join the weekly games. To your surprise, the white crewmen and the Buffalo Soldiers start getting along better. The crewmen begin to work alongside the soldiers, even shairing tools. The mean attitudes and name-calling stop.

At the end of the summer, the tensions among the Black and white crew members aren't entirely gone, but they've improved.

Tom even shakes your hand. "I'm sorry for how I treated you before," he says. "You're a good man."

THE END

To follow another path, turn to page 9.
To learn more about Buffalo Soldiers, turn to page 103.

Your job is to build this road, not antagonize the crew. You call to another Buffalo Soldier.

"Take this message to camp," you order. "Tell them Tom needs assistance."

The young Black man nods and disappears. You get back to work.

A few days later, Captain Young comes to inspect your progress. He's not happy with the speed of construction.

"This road must be done by August," he says.

You nod, but inside, you start to panic. That means building more than 10 miles of road in only a few weeks! You gather the crew and tell them your orders. No one thinks it can be done, but you have no choice.

Crews work from dawn until nightfall every day. It's a struggle to get enough water and supplies. Each week, several men pass out from the heat. Tempers grow short as the men are worked to exhaustion. But the road progresses at an amazing pace.

Finally, by August, the road is finished! It stretches for 11 miles, from the General Grant Tree all the way to Moro Rock, a huge, spectacular granite rock.

Captain Young is impressed. "This group of soldiers and civilians worked harder and built more road in two months than other crews have done in the past two years combined," he announces in a speech.

Your heart bursts with pride. It's an amazing feeling to think that you helped build something that will be part of this beautiful place forever.

THE END

To follow another path, turn to page 9.
To learn more about Buffalo Soldiers, turn to page 103.

Each day, patrolling teams set off to ride through different areas. The park itself covers more than 600 square miles of breathtaking forests, mountains, and meadows.

Sometimes you pair up with another Buffalo Soldier. Other days, you to ride out alone.

After a week of working in teams, Captain Young calls you together. "I need volunteers for two patrols," he announces.

"What jobs do you need done, sir?" you ask.

"One patrol will check a few meadows for illegal sheep grazing. The other patrol will look for poachers." He eyes your group. "Make no mistake, both assignments are dangerous. Some locals are determined to drive us out of the park for good. Watch yourselves out there."

- To check meadows for illegal grazing, go to page 67.
- To go to an area where poachers have been reported, turn to page 71.

Although the park was created to preserve the sequoia trees, they aren't the only remarkable natural areas. Dozens of untouched mountain meadows are scattered throughout the park. Illegal grazing could destroy all that beauty, and you're determined to make sure that doesn't happen.

You spend the first day visiting several mountain meadows. Wildflowers are in full bloom, and the green meadows are a riot of color.

As you approach a hard-to-find meadow, the sound of bleating sheep carries on the breeze. Your stomach drops when you see a white man sitting on a rock. His flock is grazing on a green hill.

You know that he knows he's not supposed to be here. Your job is to arrest him for illegally allowing his sheep to graze. Or perhaps reasoning with him is a better idea.

- To arrest the man, turn to page 68.
- To talk to him, turn to page 69.

You know you have to do your duty.

"Hello, sir," you greet him. "I'm afraid grazing is not allowed in the park. I must take you to see my superior officer, Captain Charles Young. He's the park superintendent"

The man eyes you warily, and you slide your hand toward your weapon.

"No one's taking me anywhere," the man says. He whips out a gun and fires.

Searing pain explodes in your side as you topple off your horse. The man jumps on your mount and gallops away, scattering the sheep.

You try to get up, but your body feels like a dead weight. Blood covers the bright green grass as you bleed to death under the bright California sky.

THE END

To follow another path, turn to page 9.
To learn more about Buffalo Soldiers, turn to page 103.

"What do you want?" the man says.

"We both know it's illegal to graze your sheep here," you begin. "Do you know why?"

"Yeah," the man replies. "The government wants us settlers and farmers to suffer!"

"Overgrazing these meadows causes a lot of damage," you say. "You've seen your own fields go brown and patchy, haven't you?"

The man looks surprised. "That's why I bring my sheep here," he replies. "Clean, sweet grass."

"It is now. But if these sheep graze here for too long, these mountain meadows will die, just like those fields," you say. "Not only that, but sheep clear out the native plants, which are food for wild animals like deer and elk."

The man looks thoughtful, so you continue. "The sheep compact the ground when they walk

Turn the page.

on it. Native trees and plants can't grow in such hard dirt. And when your sheep trample the creeks, the mud fouls the water. That kills fish and other wildlife."

You pause. "We're trying to keep the park healthy for all Americans. Maybe you can move your flock outside the park boundaries?"

The man looks shocked. "So you're not going to arrest me?"

You shake your head. "Not today. But don't let me catch you again."

With a shout, the white man rounds up his flock and herds them out of sight. Maybe he'll listen to you. Maybe he won't. Either way, today you did your duty to protect the park.

THE END

To follow another path, turn to page 9.
To learn more about Buffalo Soldiers, turn to page 103.

You and another Buffalo Soldier spend a quiet morning riding through the forest. When you come across a bubbling brook, you dismount to refill your canteens. You're about to continue the patrol when a gunshot echoes through the forest.

"Poachers," you say.

The other soldier nods. "Gotta be. Where did the shot come from?"

You pause. "I think it came from the east, near that big rocky outcropping," you say finally.

Your fellow soldier shakes his head. "I think it came from deeper in those woods there," he says, pointing.

It's not a good idea to split up. Poachers often work in groups. A lone soldier would be outnumbered. But which way should you go?

- To ride deeper into the woods, turn to page 72.
- To investigate the rocky outcropping, turn to page 78.

The giant sequoia trees at Sequoia National Park are the tallest trees in the world.

Quickly, you move deeper into the woods. You finally reach a small clearing ringed by giant sequoia trees. In the center, two men bend over the carcass of a huge elk. Anger wells up inside you at the sight.

There may be more poachers nearby. You could hide and see if others show up. Or you could sneak up on the two who are here now.

- To watch and wait, go to page 73.
- To sneak up on them, turn to page 75.

You watch from behind a sequoia tree as the men butcher the elk. They take only the best parts and leave the rest to rot. What a terrible waste!

As they pack up the fresh meat, you decide they're probably working alone. You nod silently to your partner and together you jump out, weapons drawn.

"By the authority of the United States Army, you're under arrest!" you shout.

At that moment, another poacher bursts out of the woods. He points a rifle straight at you! Shots explode all around as you run for cover. Bark flies as bullets hit the trees.

Two of the poachers disappear. A moan comes from the underbrush. You find your partner and one of the poachers lying on the ground, covered in blood.

Turn the page.

"I'm fine," your partner says as you help him up. He nods to the poacher. "This is all his blood. He got caught in the crossfire."

The poacher isn't moving. You check for a pulse but don't find one. You shake your head sadly. Such a terrible ending, and all for a few pounds of meat.

Grimly, you and your partner collect the evidence and tie the man's body to your horse. This is not how you wanted this day to go. But maybe this will send a message to other would-be poachers. The U.S. Army is serious about protecting the park and the wildlife in it.

THE END

To follow another path, turn to page 9.
To learn more about Buffalo Soldiers, turn to page 103.

You circle the clearing, slowly sneaking up on the poachers. Your partner points to some thick bushes. You spot another poacher, carefully hidden. He's cradling a rifle. It doesn't appear that he's seen you.

Your partner creeps toward the bushes. You watch, hand on your own weapon, as he gets closer. Then he silently raises his gun to the poacher's temple.

"Don't move or speak," he whispers, cocking the hammer.

The poacher freezes. Your partner takes the man's gun and ties a rag over his mouth.

Now it's your turn. Crouching, you move through the underbrush toward the others. Step, pause. Step, pause.

Just then, a twig cracks under your boot. You stop, holding your breath.

Turn the page.

The poachers jump up and frantically look around the clearing.

"Did you hear that?" one asks.

The other one grabs his gun. "I sure did."

You stay frozen and hope they don't see you. After a moment, the poachers relax.

"Must have been a squirrel or something," the gun-toting one says, putting away his gun. Soon they're back at work butchering the elk.

A stag elk in California

You jump out and run toward them. "Hands in the air! You're under arrest!" you shout.

The men whirl around and drop their tools. They curse as you tie their hands. Together, you and your partner hoist the poachers on to the horses and collect their weapons.

The men struggle and spit at you, but you merely smile, pointing your gun at one of them.

"I wouldn't try escaping if I were you," you say casually. "Us Buffalo Soldiers are trained to hit moving targets, if you know what I mean."

That quiets the poachers. Your partner chuckles as you turn toward camp. Once there, Captain Young will decide what to do with them. You've done your job.

THE END

To follow another path, turn to page 9.
To learn more about Buffalo Soldiers, turn to page 103.

You follow your gut and ride closer to the rocky outcropping. You find a small camp hidden near a cliff. There's blood and animal fur on the ground. A whisp of smoke rises from an abandoned fire.

"Poachers were here," you say, kicking the ashes.

"Looks like they left in a hurry," your partner adds.

The two of you search the camp for any clues. You spot some dried blood on a nearby rock. A faint trail leads into the forest.

"They must have gone this way," you say.

"That's old blood," your partner replies. "If it was left by the poachers, they're long gone by now."

He's probably right. The trail is cold. You could return to camp and make your report. Or you could follow the blood trail, just in case.

- To follow the blood trail, go to page 79.
- To go back to camp, turn to page 83.

You see faint bloodstains on the trees and grass as you move deeper into the forest. Then the wind changes, and the smell of smoke hits you. There's a fire somewhere in the forest!

Forest fires are one of the biggest natural threats to the park. An unchecked fire can destroy thousands of acres of wilderness.

You gallop over a small hill and stop in shock. All the trees—including the giant sequoias—have been cut down. The only thing left are enormous stumps and piles of splintered wood.

Amid the devastation, you spot the source of the smoke. A small wildfire is burning. You hear shouting, and several figures run from the fire and disappear into the forest.

"Should we go after them?" your partner yells.

"No!" you shout, fear rising in your throat. "Save the forest first!"

Turn the page.

You and your partner beat the flames with your uniform coats. Smoke stings your eyes and burns your throat. Suddenly you stumble on the uneven ground and topple into the flames!

"Help!" you shout, rolling away from the flames as you were trained to do.

Thankfully, your partner is there. He drags you to safety.

"That was close," you pant, getting to your feet. "Keep going!"

Your arms go numb as you beat the flames. Finally, you put out the fire. You're lucky that you got to the fire before it had spread very far. When you're sure there's no more flames, you and your partner sink to the charred ground. You're both covered in soot and sweat, but you're alive.

"Why would poachers set this fire?" the other soldier asks in disgust.

"Who knows?" you reply. "Maybe they tried to cover their crimes and the fire got away with them. It could have been much worse with all this dead wood and brush around."

Your partner looks around. "What is this place anyway?"

"This must be the place Captain Young told me about," you begin. "Years ago, before this became a park, a lumber company owned this land. They cut down all the sequoia trees and sold them as lumber."

Sadness squeezes your chest as you gaze at the stumps, knowing how majestic those trees must have been. You will never understand how anyone could destroy something so beautiful.

"Thank goodness someone had the good sense to get rid of that company," your partner says. You couldn't agree more.

Turn the page.

Stumps and burned trees after a fire at Sequoia National Forest

By now it's almost dark.

"Let's head back to camp," your partner says.

Wearily, you check to make sure the fire is completely out. Then you mount and start back to camp. You didn't catch the poachers, but you saved the park.

THE END

To follow another path, turn to page 9.
To learn more about Buffalo Soldiers, turn to page 103.

The trail back to camp winds through shadowy groves of trees and colorful meadows. At the edge of a ridge, you stop and gaze at the view.

Snow-capped mountains rise to the sky. Unspoiled wilderness stretches as far as you can see. The view is so overwhelmingly beautiful that you can't move or speak for some time.

Your partner is just as moved as you are. "It sure is something, isn't it?" he whispers.

You both sit in awed silence until the sun begins to set, casting the mountains in a deep purple glow. As you turn for camp, you make a silent vow—while you're here, you'll do everything you can to protect this park. And you'll remember this moment for the rest of your life.

THE END

To follow another path, turn to page 9.
To learn more about Buffalo Soldiers, turn to page 103.

CHAPTER 4

COURAGE DURING WORLD WAR I

You come from a long line of military veterans. Your grandfather was born into slavery but escaped in 1864. He joined the Union Army during the Civil War. Your father served as a Buffalo Soldier in the Spanish-American War. He also spent the summer of 1903 guarding Yosemite National Park with his regiment. Now it's 1918, and the Great War rages in Europe.

For years the U.S. refused to get involved in the war between Germany and the Allies of Great Britain, France, and Italy. But last year German submarines started attacking U.S.

Turn the page.

ships. President Woodrow Wilson declared war on Germany, and the U.S. joined the Allied Forces.

After basic training at Camp Sherman in Ohio, your all-Black army regiment is shipped to France to join the fighting. Your regiment takes the official name Buffalo Soldiers. Every soldier proudly sews a buffalo patch on his uniform.

Excitement fills you on the trip across the ocean. You can't wait to fight as a true Buffalo Soldier. But to your disappointment, your regiment is assigned boring labor such as unloading ships. Rumors swirl thorugh the ranks that the U.S. Army doesn't think Black soldiers are tough enough or smart enough to fight. Assigning Black regiments to low-level support jobs is the army's way of keeping Black soldiers away from real battle.

After weeks of loading supplies and digging latrines, you hear the French Army is in desperate need of reinforcements. They have been fighting the Germans since the war began in 1914 and have lost more than a million soldiers from death or disease. Their surviving soldiers are exhausted. General Pershing, the leader of the U.S. forces, agrees to "lend" the Buffalo Soldier regiments to the French. You're going to the front after all!

At first you're worried the white French soldiers won't accept Black troops, either. But to your surprise, the French treat you with respect. After several weeks of training, it's time to go into battle. The Allies are about to launch the largest assault of the war, the Meuse-Argonne Offensive.

You're not sure where the Buffalo Soldiers division will be sent. You could go to the front and fight in the trenches. Or you could face the German Army in the dangerous, rugged Meuse-Argonne forest.

- To fight on the front lines, turn to page 88.
- To face the enemy in the Meuse-Argonne forest, turn to page 95.

The front lines are a series of deep trenches dug into the muddy ground. The long, deep ditch helps protects you during battle. The sides are built up with sandbags, wooden planks, or sticks. But when it rains, the trenches become pits of stinking mud. The filthy conditions cause sickness and disease. You spend your days knee-deep in mud, shooting at the enemy. At night, you sleep sitting up against a muddy trench wall.

You have no idea what will happen each day. Some are quiet. On others, the Germans shower you with bombs and gunfire. You've watched fellow soldiers torn to pieces right in front of you. You know that any minute, you could be next.

One morning, *BOOM!* You wake to a huge explosion that shakes the trench. German airplanes whine overhead as they fly over, dropping bombs.

Black soldiers wait for combat in a muddy trench during World War I.

You can barely get into position before the attack is fully underway. *BOOM!* Another bomb hits. A wall collapses, burying several soldiers. Pain shoots up your leg as blood seeps from a shrapnel wound. It hurts, but it doesn't look too bad. You could get a medic to take a look. Or you can keep fighting.

- To find a medic, turn to page 90.
- To keep fighting, turn to page 91.

You could lose your leg—or die—if you don't find a medic. You limp as fast as you can through the trench to the aid station. It's filled with injured soldiers.

You wait for hours. Finally, an exhausted medic dresses your wound. You're transported to nearby field hospital and placed in an all-Black medical tent.

A Black doctor gently cares for you. "There are only a handful of us in the army," he tells you. "We're not allowed to work with white troops."

Despite the care, your wound gets infected. Doctors have no choice but to amputate your leg. A few weeks later, a nurse pushes your wheelchair to the transport ship home. You say a silent goodbye to France and your brief military career.

THE END

To follow another path, turn to page 9.
To learn more about Buffalo Soldiers, turn to page 103.

You tie a cloth around the wound and keep shooting. A German airplane crashes into the ground, nose-first. You scored a hit!

The battle rages for several days, but neither side is successful. When the Germans finally retreat, nothing seems to have changed. The good news is your wound heals with no infection. You got lucky.

Soon after the battle, the French generals order the troops to move. You don't know why, but it doesn't matter. You must obey orders. Every soldier—Black and white alike—is exhausted from fear, constant battle, and lack of sleep.

Wearily, you strap on your heavy pack and begin the march. Most roads have been ripped apart by bombs. The rest are blocked by abandoned equipment. It's clear that the guns, tanks, and supply trucks can't get through.

Turn the page.

General Pershing is standing with a group of senior officers. "We've got to get a road built here," he barks. "Have the men get to work immediately!"

Your commanding officer gathers the troops. You've learned enough French by now to understand what he's saying.

"The U.S. general wants a road built as fast as possible," he announces. "But some of you must stay with the guns in case the Germans attack again."

You can help with the road work. Or you can stay with the heavy artillery.

- To work on the road, turn to page 93.
- To stay with the guns, turn to page 94.

You and the road crew work each night as the rest of the troops defend against German attacks. Each night, enemy planes drop bombs all around. Flashes from gunfire light up the dark sky. The roar of battle fills the air. Soldiers fall all around you. Some are only injured. Others die. You swallow your terror and focus on the work at hand.

On the third night, you hear the high-pitched whistle of an artillery shell overhead. Before you can react, it explodes, throwing you into the air. You land hard, bones breaking. Strangely, there's no pain. You watch the lights of battle in the sky as your life ebbs away in a muddy French field.

THE END

To follow another path, turn to page 9.
To learn more about Buffalo Soldiers, turn to page 103.

You and your fellow troops dig shallow trenches and pull the guns into position. As night falls, you hear the roar of German airplanes. The sky lights with streaks of gunfire. Your ears ring with deafening explosions as bombs rain down.

For three nights, the Germans relentlessly attack. The Buffalo Soldiers and the French forces return fire. Late on the third night, the sky grows quiet. Your heart leaps with hope. You've won!

Suddenly a chemical smell fills the air. It's a mustard gas attack! The deadly chemical weapon was invented by the Germans. Cheers turn to screams as the men scramble to find their gas masks. You frantically reach for yours, but it's gone. Your lungs burn with the poison. You collapse, losing consciousness as you die, gasping for breath.

THE END

To follow another path, turn to page 9.
To learn more about Buffalo Soldiers, turn to page 103.

The Allied Army battles its way through the Meuse-Argonne forest. You're under constant attack by German forces.

One night, you're assigned sentry duty at a station in the forest. It's about a mile or so away from the main camp. Roberts, another Buffalo Soldier, joins you but dozes off while waiting for replacements. Your eyes get heavy too.

Suddenly, you jerk awake and grab for your weapon. What woke you up?

An owl hoots nearby. That must have been it, you think.

But then you hear a rustling noise nearby. It might be the owl hunting, but you're not sure. You could ignore it. Or you could wake Roberts.

• To ignore the sound, turn to page 96.
• To wake Roberts, turn to page 97.

You can't be afraid of every little sound. These dense woods are filled with the calls and rustlings of animals and insects every night. You're sure you'll know the sound of a real attack when it comes.

Two replacements finally arrive. You and Roberts stumble through the dark woods back toward camp. Before you make it, someone grabs you from behind. A German soldier!

You open your mouth to shout, but the enemy claps his hand over your mouth and slides a knife into your side. He drops you on the ground and disappears into the darkness. The last thing you hear before you bleed to death is shouting and gunfire from the surprise German attack.

THE END

To follow another path, turn to page 9.
To learn more about Buffalo Soldiers, turn to page 103.

You shake Roberts awake. Then you hear a soft clipping noise. Someone is cutting the barbed wire that's been strung around the perimeter.

"Throw a grenade," you whisper to Roberts.

He nods and throws. The explosion lights up the darkness and reveals figures crouched near the barbed wire. It's a sneak German attack!

There's a burst of gunfire and explosions. You and Roberts throw grenade after grenade.

Finally, everything goes silent. Maybe it's over. It's a good thing too. All you have left is one French rifle, some American-made ammunition, and a large combat knife.

Then a shot rings out. Roberts falls on the ground. He's seriously wounded and needs medical help. But there might still be German soldiers waiting in the dark.

• To go for help, turn to page 98.
• To stay in the trench, turn to page 99.

Moving quietly, you crawl out of the trench and stand. *BOOM!* A grenade blast throws you to the ground. You lift your head and see German soldiers swarming the trench where you left Roberts. Then a bullet hits you in the chest, and you collapse. You wake up in a field hospital.

"The German sneak attack failed," your commanding officer tells you. "You made a brave choice leaving when you did."

You don't feel brave. You're wracked with guilt over leaving Roberts. Even the knowledge that you likely would have died too doesn't help.

You're sent home with honors. You try to put the war behind you, but your carry this sadness— and the memory of your friend—for the rest of your life.

THE END

To follow another path, turn to page 9.
To learn more about Buffalo Soldiers, turn to page 103.

You can't leave Roberts. As a last resort, you grab the American-made ammunition and shove it into your French rifle. But when you pull the trigger, nothing happens. The gun jams!

Panic grips you as German soldiers jump into the trench. You race toward them, slamming their heads with the wooden rifle butt. One soldier goes down, then another. You lose all sense of time as you fight off enemy soldiers. Bullets hit your side and graze your head, but you ignore the pain.

You hit one German so hard that your rifle butt breaks. He collapses, but there are more behind him. Roberts cries out as German soldiers try to drag him out of the trench. A large German soldier drops into the trench near you. You have to decide whether to help Roberts or deal with the German soldier.

- To rescue Roberts, turn to page 100.
- To attack the soldier, turn to page 101.

Black Soldiers won several French medals for the bravery they showed in battle.

Turning, you stumble over a fallen German soldier and lose your balance. This gives the enemy his chance. Two shots ring out, and you fall to the ground, wounded. The enemy soldiers shoot your friend and leave you to die in the trench, another casualty of this terrible war.

THE END

To follow another path, turn to page 9.
To learn more about Buffalo Soldiers, turn to page 103.

You lunge at the soldier, slashing with your combat knife. He goes down. More German soldiers appear, and you keep up the attack. Finally, there are none left.

You stay with Roberts until reinforcements arrive. You've suffered more than a dozen wounds, but you'll live. The next day, a group of French and U.S. officers visit you in the hospital tent. They tell you your bravery stopped the German Army from breaking through the French lines.

When the war is over, the French Army awards you and Roberts the Croix de Guerre avec Palme, their highest miliary award for valor. You're the first U.S. soldiers to get this honor. You return to the U.S. a hero, one of the finest Buffalo Soldiers who ever served.

THE END

To follow another path, turn to page 9.
To learn more about Buffalo Soldiers, turn to page 103.

CHAPTER 5

THE LEGACY OF BUFFALO SOLDIERS

For more than 80 years, Buffalo Soldiers served—and died—for the United States. Despite overwhelming racial prejudice, Buffalo Soldiers proved their courage through some of the world's bloodiest conflicts. Many have been recognized as heroes for their bravery and valor.

Captain Charles Young was one such soldier. Born in 1864 to enslaved parents, Young was accepted into West Point Military Academy in 1884. He was only the ninth Black student to attend. Upon graduation, Young became an officer in the Ninth Cavalry Buffalo Soldiers. There, he rose to the rank of captain. During the summer of

1903, he and his Buffalo Soldier regiment were sent to Sequoia and General Grant National Parks to protect the new park and build roads and trails. Young is considered to be the first Black national park superintendent. The trails he and his Buffalo Soldiers built are still used today.

Edward Lee Baker Jr. was born free in 1865 and grew up in Wyoming. He joined the Ninth Cavalry Buffalo Soldiers when he was only 16 years old. In a few years, he rose to the rank of sergeant major. Sergeant Major Baker and his Buffalo soldier regiment fought in the Spanish-American War in 1898. During one fierce battle, Baker risked his life to save a fellow soldier from drowning. For this courageous act, he was awarded the Medal of Honor in 1902.

Henry Johnson, born in 1892, enlisted in the U.S. Army in 1917. His Buffalo Soldier regiment fought with the French Army during

World War I. One night on sentry duty, Johnson and another Buffalo Soldier were attacked by German soldiers. Johnson ran out of ammunition and engaged in hand-to-hand combat. When the Germans tried to capture the other injured soldier, Johnson attacked with his knife. Although he suffered 21 wounds, Johnson survived. The French Army awarded him its highest military honor, the Croix de Guerre avec Palme.

Despite loyally serving their country, most Buffalo Soldiers in the U.S. faced discrimination and hostility after their service was over. Most did not receive the recognition they deserved until long after their deaths. Captain Charles Young was abruptly discharged from the U.S. Army and spent years trying to return. In 2022—100 years after Young's death—President Joe Biden recognized his service by posthumously promoting him to Brigadier General.

Henry Johnson was discharged soon after World War I ended. Although he was a war hero, he couldn't find work because of his injuries. He died in 1929, forgotten and penniless. Years later, in 1996, President Bill Clinton posthumously awarded Johnson a Purple Heart. In 2015, President Barak Obama awarded Johnson the Medal of Honor.

Buffalo Soldiers faced unimaginable odds. They fought in wars, protected people on the frontier, and preserved parks, all while experiencing hate and discrimination. But they persevered with courage and determination. By World War II, the U.S. military could no longer ignore their patriotism and sacrifice. In 1948, the army desegregated the military. The all-Black Buffalo Soldier regiments were abolished. Today, soldiers of all races serve their country together. And the stories—and bravery—of the Buffalo Soldiers of the past continue to be honored today.

Buffalo Soldiers Timeline

1865: The Civil War ends. Slavery is abolished.

1866: The United States Army creates six permanent all-Black regiments.

1867-1896: Buffalo Soldiers serve throughout the American West, including in Texas, Arizona, Wyoming, and California

1869: The six all-Black regiments are consolidated into four: the Ninth and Tenth Cavalry and the 24th and 25th Infantry.

1884: Charles Young, future captain, is admitted to West Point, the United States military academy, as a cadet.

1898: Buffalo Soldiers serve in the Spanish-American War.

1899-1902: Buffalo Soldiers see battle in the Philippine-American War.

1903: A regiment of Buffalo Soldiers, led by Captain Charles Young, is assigned to guard Sequoia, Yosemite, and General Grant National Parks. Captain Young becomes the first Black park superintendent.

1916: Buffalo Soldier regiments are sent to Mexico to capture Mexican revolutionary leader Pancho Villa.

1917: The U.S. enters World War I; more than 350,000 Black soldiers serve.

1918: World War I ends.

1938: World War II begins in Europe.

1941: The United States enters World War II; more than one million Black men and women serve.

1945: World War II ends.

1948: President Harry S. Truman signs Executive Order 9981, desegregating the United States Armed Forces.

1951: The 24th Infantry, the last official Buffalo Soldier regiment, is dissolved.

2005: Mark Matthews (b. 1894), the oldest living Buffalo Soldier, dies at age 111. He is buried at Arlington National Cemetery.

Other Paths to Explore

1. You're a Buffalo Soldier sent to a fort in the West. You have one main job: support the U.S. government in rounding up Indigenous people and forcing them onto reservations. You know what the government is trying to do is wrong. But you're a proud United States soldier, ready to serve his country. How can you balance your love of country with your outrage at the terrible treatment of the Indigenous nations?

2. The first time you see Yosemite's Monument Valley, the beauty takes your breath away. But others only value the land for the resources it provides to people. Trees are meant to be used for building. Land is meant for growing crops. People need plants and animals for food. Industries such as mining create jobs. To them, preserving any land is a waste. Especially here, in an area so remote that few tourists will ever visit. Is protecting a beautiful landscape simply for the view more important than providing food, shelter, and jobs?

3. As a Buffalo Soldier in World War I, you served alongside white French soldiers. They treated you no differently than anyone else. After the war ends, you spend time in Paris and other French towns. For the first time in your life, you can freely go anywhere. There are no signs telling Black people they aren't welcome. You don't have to use back doors when you enter a building. Restaurants and shops don't refuse to serve you. You want to live like this forever, simply to be treated like a human being. But you miss your friends and family. What is worth more: a life of freedom from prejudice and hate, or being close to the love and support of family?

Bibliography

*Army Historical Foundation: Fighting for Respect:
African-American Soldiers in WWII*
armyhistory.org/fighting-for-respect-african-american-
soldiers-in-wwi/

History: Buffalo Soldiers
history.com/topics/19th-century/buffalo-soldiers

*National Museum of African American History and Culture:
Buffalo Soldiers*
nmaahc.si.edu/explore/stories/buffalo-soldiers

National Museum of the United States Army: Buffalo Soldiers
thenmusa.org/articles/buffalo-soldiers/

National Park Service: Buffalo Soldiers:
nps.gov/chyo/learn/historyculture/buffalo-soldiers.htm#:
~:text=AmericanPlainsIndianswhofoughtAmerican
regimentsformedin1866

*National World War I Museum and Memorial: Firsthand
Accounts from Black Soldiers in WWI*
theworldwar.org/learn/about-wwi/black-soldiers-wwi

The Negro Combat Division
net.lib.byu.edu/estu/wwi/comment/scott/SCh11.htm

Yosemite: Buffalo Soldiers of Yosemite
yosemite.com/the-buffalo-soldiers-of-yosemite/

Glossary

apprehensive (aa-prih-HEN-siv)—fearful of what may be coming

artery (AR-tuh-ree)—a large blood vessel that carries blood away from the heart

artillery (ar-TIH-luh-ree)—guns or missile launchers that can be moved

desegregate (dee-SEH-grih-gayt)—to end racial separation

desolate (DEH-suh-luht)—lacking signs of life

discrimination (dih-skrih-muh-NAY-shuhn)—treating people badly based on the group they belong to instead of as individuals

grenade (gruh-NAYD)—a small explosive device that is thrown

Indigenous (in-DIH-juh-nuhs)—people who are the original, earliest inhabitants of an area

posthumously (POS-chuh-muhs-lee)—after a person's death

prejudice (PREJ-uh-diss)—a negative opinion of someone without knowing the facts

regiment (REJ-uh-muhnt)—a military unit made of several battalions

reservation (rez-er-VAY-shuhn)—an area of land set aside for Indigenous nations to live

sentry (SEN-tree)—a guard

shrapnel (SHRAP-nuhl)—pieces that have broken off from an explosive shell

Read More

Herschbach, Elisabeth. *Black Soldiers in the Civil War.* Lake Elmo, MN: Focus Readers, 2020.

Lake, Theia. *Buffalo Soldiers.* New York: PowerKids Press, 2024.

Tyner, Artika R. *The Courageous Six Triple Eight: The All-Black Female Batallion of World War II.* North Mankato, MN: Capstone Press, 2023.

Internet Sites

Academic Kids: Buffalo Soldier
https://academickids.com/encyclopedia/index.php/Buffalo_soldiers

Kiddle: Buffalo Soldier Facts for Kids
https://kids.kiddle.co/Buffalo_Soldier

National Museum of African American History & Culture: Buffalo Soldiers
https://nmaahc.si.edu/explore/stories/buffalo-soldiers

Yosemite: The Buffalo Soldiers of Yosemite
https://www.yosemite.com/the-buffalo-soldiers-of-yosemite/

JOIN OTHER HISTORICAL ADVENTURES WITH MORE YOU CHOOSE SEEKING HISTORY!

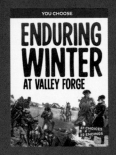

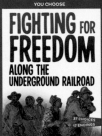

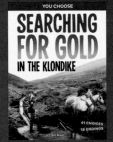

About the Author

Allison Lassieur is the award-winning author of more than 150 historical and nonfiction books about everything from ancient Rome to the International Space Station. Her books have received several Kirkus starred reviews and Booklist recommendations, and her historical novel *Journey to a Promised Land* was awarded the 2020 Kansas Library Association Notable Book Award and Library of Congress Great Reads Book selection. Allison lives in upstate New York with her husband, daughter, a scruffy, lovable mutt named Jingle Jack, and more books than she can count.